...AND SO, THE WIND WAS BORN

Gina Duran

FlowerSong Press
McAllen, Texas 78501

ISBN: 978-1-953447-73-9
Library of Congress Number: 2021933495

Published by FlowerSong Press
in the United States of America.
www.flowersongpress.com

Set in Adobe Garamond Pro

Cover art by
Typeset and design by Matthew Revert
www.matthewrevert.com

GRATITUDE

Thank you to Edward Vidaurre, for believing in my work as a writer and poet. This is a dream come true and an honor to work with you on this project. I am so grateful to you and your dream—FlowerSong Press.

Thank you to Matt Sedillo, for valuing me as a poet and introducing me to Edward and FlowerSong Press, and for welcoming me into a world with inspiring Latinx and Chicanx poets—such as yourself, Edward, and many others.

Thank you to Jo Reyes-Boitel for your kind edits and discussions about our shared love for commas. You are so appreciated.

Thank you to Brent Armendinger, for all your encouragement of this project, for helping me finish a dream, and sharing your passion for poetry and words. I will forever be cognizant of the shapes and sounds of letters forming from my mouth to the page, because of you.

Thank you to Michelle Dowd, who inspired me to go after my dreams as a poet and encouraged me to submit and publish February 5th, in the Chaffey Review, Volume XIII. You are a catalyst of change and a loving friend.

Thank you to Mon Coeur, who has ignited the changes in my life that have given me strength to wake up and pursue my degrees when I thought I lost everything. We began our journey with *Twenty-One Love Poems: XIII*, by Adrienne Rich and I learned that endings are beginnings, and we have just begun. You have held my hand through hurricanes—then danced in the pouring rain and over painted stars with me. I am captivated.
(This book is a Lunch Box Message).

TABLE OF CONTENTS

Chapter 1

...and so, the Wind was Born

The Healer's Market

He said I was like the wind.
I wondered if he saw
Mon Coeur. I said that the wind
did tend to appear in my life
a lot. Sometimes it told me
when people were near.
He asked me my sign.

Aquarius.

That kind of wind—as if learning something
intrinsically important about me. *You are like
a sandstorm. In a good way.*

Maybe I am the wind.
Maybe that's why it speaks to me.
In hushed tones to my vellus—as it fills up my heart chakra.
Maybe the wind twirling her skirt is my anahata
saying this is someone you love.
Maybe I am the whirlwind that people tell me to be
careful of.
My ribs are cracked, exposing the chambers in my chest.
But what if I am the whirlwind that people are
mindful of?
Maybe I am careful of me.
Maybe I need to hear the wind—not the words.

Fontana is Where the Winds Destroyed Everything

Fontana is where the valley lied
between the hills and mountains

Tiny dirt devils twirl in
tumbleweed paths
Loose gravel flings about as mini
tornadoes feverishly shred papers in
school yards and shoot out

the brittle golden thorns that
cling to socks and shoes
stabbing the soles of feet

Fontana is where the Santa Ana Winds
thrive by devouring rooftops and tree roots

They howl and screech with fury in the night
disguising the screams behind wrought iron gates
and hiding in the corners where oxygen leaves

lungs wet with tears masked by smiles

The Santa Ana Winds move trash in the night
They sound like fists knocking on the door at 2am

They thrive from the hot air and swirl like the madness
contained in the barrel of a pistol of a teenage gangbanger

looming under a large oak tree

on the lawn of a high school taking cover
With piercing screams thrashing through leaves

The Santa Ana Winds rush down the halls
slapping doors open and kicking dirt on the tile
They slide under tennis shoes and screams of

gunmen running by

The Santa Ana Winds rush past all the new buildings
that once had fields with horses trotting through
grape vineyards and kumquat trees where

stalkers sleep

The Santa Ana Winds roll giant tumbleweeds
across junkyards with meth heads who sell drugs
to teenage girls who drop out of school for their

next fix

The Santa Ana Winds smack mirrored blinds
against windows while a mother kicks her daughter in the gut

The Santa Ana Winds leave her lungs as she falls
down the steps onto the laundry room floor

The Santa Ana Winds bang against bodies
like a 10 year old girl being beaten by a door torn
off the hinges

The Santa Ana Winds rush to tear away the shingles of the house
when a 17 year old girl gets raped by her boyfriend
but she only remembers

saying no

The Santa Ana Winds witness her frail 27 year old
body flatten to the concrete in Riverside

The Santa Ana Winds wrap over and around her
rushing into her lungs as people step over her body
laying under the February sun

The Santa Ana Winds encase her and escape
between her lips as she mumbles incoherently to paramedics

The Santa Ana Winds reek of her black charcoaled vomit
all over her hospital gown and creep up her slip as she enters
her coma state

The Santa Ana Winds witness
when she left her remains and took her last breath

Her son and daughter stared out the window
as the sun sizzles and pops beneath the ocean waves
and the moon peeks through the clouds—

forever dreaming of winds altering stars and memories

The next day a breeze lay tucked into the sheets
as she gathered her heat to gain momentum
ready to meet something other than the Santa Ana Winds

Fire and Wind

fire is a common occurrence. fire is a common occurrence
in California and the power of the Santa Ana
Winds

decimate, evaporate
dissipate the green through a straw
like a greedy child with sticky hands

fire is a common occurrence. fire is a common occurrence
amongst the brittle drought ridden weeds
where

field mice and gophers scurry, play
frolic in the kumquat trees and birds
flutter quick as dogs run free down

empty roads like Almond, Cypress, Banana,
and Jurupa where a long stretch of gravel
begins to roll with the hills

as a Pitta girl called to the wind while falling
to her knees

begging Jesus in the cleft of the south east corner
of her hot pink carpeted room

in the silence the wind emptied from her lungs
raging the sizzles and chews of flames

in the silence. in the silence a puff of dirt alerts
when visitors pass. In the silence the wind
cries between the windowpane

tapping Christmas lights against the frame

under the tinseled tree is a stretched blue
knitted sweater newly worn and thrown

across the living room floor
of a swollen lipped and purple faced
girl

in the silence God is not questioned
and dad's heavy calloused hands

build bridges and skyscrapers to futures
where high winds are God

and blue-collar Catholics spend seven am
Sundays giving gratitude for cushioned
falls

but in the silence fire devours everything

as a young girl screams but no
one does a thing

in the silence. in the silence the fire
is seen

but no one does a thing

Lunchbox Message:
When She Walked into the Room

I will miss her

The way she walked into the room
astonishing eyes from all points of view

I didn't look until I heard her voice
that is when I knew, I would meet her soon

Then one day the wind brought her in
like poetry on my path, as if to tell me
it was time to look within

That's when I walked into the vast

My breath was stolen from my air deprived chest
my heart beat deep beneath my breasts

And I knew that it was my last

A sublime cascade of words
Floated through me like a song

I never had a clue
That everything I thought I knew
Would sit in a silent wake of truth

Within stale, knowing, mortared walls
worlds collided, then made anew

The wind blew through
a plentiful gale of stories

Empty pages waiting for their words
from minds we have never heard

My aching heart soon brought to ease

Like the floating autumn leaves at her skirt
I never understood the swift air
within the Earth, I just know it took away the hurt

I dreamt of dancing in the rain
Deleting all the pain

That is when I go back to days past
Moments I hoped would always last

The way she walked into the room
astonishing eyes from all points of view

I didn't look until I heard her voice
that is when I knew, I would meet her soon

Then one day the wind brought her in
like poetry on my path, as if to tell me
it was time to look within

That's when I walked into the vast

Timeless, where life is all by chance

I dreamt of dancing in the rain
Deleting all the pain

Our hair wet and curled
Spinning free from all the world

Prancing stars all around us
lying deep in swaying grass

Freed from fear, whenever she was near
My heart settled in her hand with ease
Then sat in silence in a meditative trance
We struggle to have our hearts release
But she is the iridescent light pouring

Warmth along the murky furrows
On a rigid winter schedule, waiting

For the seconds, floating like a current
Springing to that moment to

The way she walked into the room
astonishing eyes from all points of view

Lunchbox Message:
Captivated

I cannot look into your eyes
or I will be captivated
in a sea
of green and flecks of gold
never wanting to return.

Eyes so gentle yet intense
sending me into a whirlwind
my mind keeps whirling and twirling
like the wind beneath your skirt.

My heart is catching on fire
beating through my swollen throat
when all I want to do is whisper
I love you.

I love you.

Instead I mutter *I am sorry*
because I am. Sorry
I could not be what you wanted.
My mind keeps whirling and twirling
like the wind beneath your skirt

and all I want to do is yell
Get out of the wind
you are too beautiful
to stand in the wind.

Instead I point and stammer
and you remain in the wind
you are too beautiful
to stand in the wind.

I cannot look into your eyes
or I will be captivated
But you are free
and all I want is you
to be free with me.

Lunchbox Message:

Season of Breaks

The window cracks
with the gale
of a heart's wake

Vibrant, bright green

glossy eyed
pain

Golden locks

milky white finger   tips

Pulling back

again

Rays of sun drops
beaded sweat

End of summer days

Beatific is her voice
with precision

Unencumbered

are my words
betwixt Winter's break

forwards, backwards,

beating, skipping, in

between

...Running...

Late night thoughts

Early morning talks

Yes, No
Maybe

Decimated shards

Spring

from these
Passing seasons

Winds and Apparitions

Cher Mon Coeur,

We are still young. Fuck age. All I have
learned from my many lives is that
I know nothing.

When I was laid on stark white sheets
of the hospital bed in my twenties—
stained with my black charcoaled vomit—

I was sure I knew everything. There I was: young,
thin, sexually confused, a woman afraid to leave

her straight life, and a girl who still obeyed
her mom. I begged my then god for forgiveness
as I wandered into a new life. The sun gnawed
at my skin and the February breeze tapped me
on the shoulder. I thought it was god, but it was my ghost.

She was fragile with sunk in eyes, pasty pale papered skin,
and purple boils on her concave cheeks—from the lithium
that helped her escape her body.

As she left I heard the voices of doctors calling our name—
but only the wind answered. I don't know what it said…
It was dark and they stripped off my ghost's clothes…

I watched them. I remember how angry she was that more
men were touching her body, but I told her to fuck off…

I wasn't ready to die. Then the wind forced me into a silent blackness
where it whispered my truths. Suddenly the earth began to spin
while the wind turned with it.

I wretched and gagged as my life's apparitions went left
and I went right. I flung up onto a metal bar and watched
the circulating black contents of my ghost's nightmares spread
across the curtains—from the Coriolis effect. She was

a cyclonic force ripping through my body—so I killed
that pilled up bitch that February 5th. Once the cyclone passed
the wind told me to be patient and that I would find you
— as it woke me in the morning—
it teased me about my nakedness. I laughed,
my ghost would have cried.

Suddenly, I felt an updraft beneath the sheets climbing gently between my legs and onto my vulva. My nipples grew hard.
Oh...that was real.
I'm naked...

Fuck, I'm naked. They all saw me...

Then the wind flung itself into my lungs—my heart
bounced and my eyes opened. The bright fluorescent
hospital lights waved across my eyes in a smear
She woke up, a voice announced. I looked to my right to see
black charcoaled attempts hanging onto the blue grey curtains.

It was real. I did that.
And for what?

The October before I stopped watching my ghost
live for me, there was the one who called herself
The Apple Temptress
—and she was intoxicating. Her soft green eyes lured
me in and told me she was the one I dreamt of when
I was a girl. The one I would dance with in the pouring
rain. She didn't even like the rain.

I don't regret kissing her. She was the first woman
my lips had known...
without her...I would still be hidden deep between
my letterman's jacket and my first
white wedding dress—
pretending to be a good Catholic girl.

She taught me that feeling male was okay
and talked about her dreams
of fucking girls as a man. She taught me about ghosts
as she snorted her crystal phantoms up her nose. She told me
how her uncle used to have all his nieces and nephews over
for drug parties when she was in junior high. A smile
flashed as she cut me a line.

I wanted to be brave. But I was used to reserving
bravery for repelling from cliffs and performing
on stage. I wanted to prove that I could be
a bad girl, that
I was sexy…

god I wanted to be sexy.

But I said I would never touch crystal…

Her uncle was like my uncles—
only mine sent bleeding apparitions with long blond hair
to my childhood home. Mine shoved bongs up the ass
of boys who grew to touch me. The Apple Temptress
had her own ghosts, ones that

only she should tell.   Ones that left her feeling like
she wasn't enough. She dyed her hair as dark as a starless sky
and insisted
it was natural. She told me
she wanted lip injections, because she could never
be beautiful enough. Her body dysmorphia sent her to the
doctor

for two unnecessary breast implant
corrections—because she wasn't
enough.
I wonder if her wind escaped her body like mine or if she
continues to haunt her children and the husband
she never loved.

She cut down the crystal three more times, then
giggled... *That's not really anything. Are you sure*
you still want to do this?

My ghost stared into her longingly—with the feeling
of never being enough.

My ghost once hid in svadhisthana, where she stored my murky
memories. She's the one
who would tell me I'm not enough—sometimes she still laughs
like the Apple Temptress and calls me stupid like my father,
frightens me like my ex-husband, and taunts me to kill myself

like my mother. But mostly...

my ghost haunts me with subtleties in the midst
of conversation or even a kiss
She reminds me that I am too much or
to give more of myself, because

my mother said it's all or nothing,
so I give the marrow from my bones
and the wind stored in my anahata until

my alveoli are deflated cheerios and
my lips shrivel into lavender petals. Then
my bones will whistle in the breeze to the tune
of my elegy,

because all my efforts toward love
will finally be more than nothing
and my all might finally be enough.

Stars in Her Eyes

Her eyes shined bright
As if there were galaxies
Of stars expanding in her
Soul

The world swirled around
Us while fragmented colors
Sparked with tawny flecked
Dust

The past felt like a wind
Passing by my knees
Flowing through my wavy
Hair

I walked down cemented
Stairs, knowing who I'd see
Stories past carried in a
Breeze

Paintings hung on walls
With manufactured dreams
Streaming high from showroom
Ceilings

Fragments of the past
Hindering their dreams
Weapons of destruction splicing
Walls

The colors of the night
Took presence in her hair
Her lips left sight of morning
Dew

Darkness reflected the moon
Like waters in a pond
Late hours took with tempted
Falls

Lunchbox Message:

Remanence of Me

I lie in my bed with the sticky
webs of memories spun round me
like golden sap which clings and oozes
from a maple tree

I think back to when I held your hand
and you kissed me on the busy street
cars fluttered the chiffon of your skirt

they rushed by as the leaves
began to scatter and plop like brisk
January rain
                    drops

We were marching with millions of women
around the world drinking up love
from water bottles and traversing the tarred
streets while breaking in new hiking boots

You said that the love was good energy for
my travels and I held your hand as we created
a chain of connection through the crowd

We came upon a meditation spot but our friends
were in a rush so I took a picture of our people
sitting in the light before the storm

The train couldn't move fast enough to tomorrow
When the plops and drips of rain on asphalt

made a melody to the beat of your heart speaking to mine
through the cage that keeps my voice contained like a whisper

that only your lips heard

But I saw you in the sunlight on a warm summer's day
when you peaked through the crevices of my
hands and kissed me again
I will never know a softer touch than yours

When you helped spin the silk around my body
I shed the pieces of my parents
which they willed
I felt safe at last I want to forget

your whispers that shushed the speeding cars
that spilled out onto the tile floor with my heart
beating next to yours *Don't hold it against me*
I realize now you were speaking from fear

I have turned to liquid flowing through the cool
cracks of the tile floor next to the shattered
fragments of my heart covered in red earth
All the pieces belong to you now

The light is so blinding it is dark inside
But I will emerge soon
I feel change with the breeze kissing my lips
like a lover fluttering across my body

Lunchbox Message:
Sunday

The sun was soft with chipped paint,
like clouds peeling from the sky
after a gentle rain

The air was brisk and your golden hair
matched the earthy reminiscent of dried
pine needles in the sprayed burnt ink

dripped container full with the pieces of

my hridaya

Followed by fallen
leaves, with the words that float
upon my page

Swirls of violet, watermelon pink, and gold
dripping teal and metallic glitter, that spark
my dreams of us under the aurora borealis

You reminded me of a painting
swirling in the citrus trees
Placing pieces of the puzzle together

I will remember the shattered glass and water
splattered across your violet toenails
sparkling flecks scattered on your ankles

The cold lava rock flopped

out from containment
bursting out onto the floor with

water spilling out like the contents
Of my heart
You always knew how to split it

open so the solid contents
became malleable like red-earth
rolling beneath the curved patterns

on your fingertips
My chest thumped and cracked my ribs
my heart begged for the air

passing over your lips

like honey

with my vertiginous dread of your disappointment
But you relaxed with the gentle green sea
glistening in your eyes

I will remember the wind of the rushing cars
while nestled in the truth of your embrace
and the soft warmth of your kisses silencing

zooms and hisses of passing engines
My mind stopped spinning and I knew
Mon Coeur was home

Un-know[1]

There is a part of me that wishes I could go back
To sleep
That wishes I could wake to sun glowing on
My rosy cheeks reddening with
The amalgamation of tears and blood
that soil the earth's mud-red earth
Before I knew about the stains the world bore
Loss of many Indigenous ancestors that knew nothing of
borders and open wounds
Not eyes

that wish to wake to sands with rolling pebbles in running rivers
Before I knew my great great grandmother was shackled
with chains in a boxcar by a man
Who I know is responsible for my tears and blood
I am a product of what was lost
And I wish to open my eyes and unsee
To not know that my great grandmother died with her
Other
brown children that she bore
beyond borders
My grandmother without a mother
never knowing that chocolate and red tanned skin
I remember her three visits before she passed
in the arms of her Mexican blood
I never knew
I want to un-know my uncle
and father
and my mother's past

It would be nice to go back to sleep
        (Without the nightmares)
Before I knew the difference between
            sessions and cessions

                                        and men named Sessions
All end with ramifications of families torn apart
Through death and prejudice
Which the They call laws for   Others
I wish I could un-see the   Othered parts of me
Who travel through treachery of tears and blood
Locked away to remain

                            un-seen
            (within) chained walls
I am seen and un-seen
        Invisible to eyes

Maybe if they wake   they will
        see the un-seen
                Me

1 Duran, Gina. "Un-know." Sexual Violence and the Assimilation Response of LGBTQ2 Female Identified Latina and Indigenous Americans. University of Illinois Urbana-Champaign. 2018. (pp 13). 2018.

Born from Anamnesis

The air is still as a pulsating heart pounds inside the wind
Blood circulating like a tornado
Writhing in the abdomen of a beast

Yet externally
it is silent as a force of gossip plunders landscapes
—the earth concaves and vexes
with imprints of the violence upon her body

Like her mother before her

With uncles' hands big or small

Friction (in the ropes—bound to memories)

Friction under a young man's hands

With her legs pried open as the darkening
vastly spreads

Tectonic plates rubbing rigidly in turmoil

Red-earth rising up
while the dreams of family
lay piled within splintered rocks

Now she is he and he is she
rooted to clay and stone
bound by anamnesis

Covered in mud
Stagnant in stases

Waves of blue flow through
swaying across the concrete floor

To find the tornado churning
captured in a well of stomach acids
with its youth

Naked

Naked and redacted from cognizance
Black tape across the gaping truth

But the erosion of its force is fierce
Its rage imperils its vessel pulsating
through the boundaries of family secrets
in a gale

A gale wreaking havoc
Meeting up with a force more powerful than itself

A love of waves birthing whirlwinds and windstorms

Clenching the tool to release the ferocity
looming in the corner
Dressed as a rainbow before the rain

Forgetting the wind knocked from its lungs
was once an updraft of bellowing breath

Before it circulated in animosity and despair
sublimating rage

Before the crystalized contents of its tears
deposited in a downdraft of

heated memories infusing the tropopause
of its phantom psyche

Its phantom psyche which nurtured
chaos
Its nurtured chaos which nourished
childhood
Stagnant musty air rising in a whisper
from the cartilage of its throat

Its eyes transfixed as spectators gathered

Swaying waves forced static
memories from the hollowed womb
of the wind

Laboring the tornado through
strained and stained mud of its ancestors
Its muscles relaxed in the familiarity
of childhood

bondage

Its muscles relaxed in the familiarity
of familial

bondage

The wind's thoughts grew rapid with
its breath

Heat
waves entering the scarred tissue
of its traumatized tropopause

shackled in a boxcar with the tornado's
great winds before it

Where the debris of violators span
across the landscape

colonizing its body

Dissociating the wind from its home

Searching
for a sense of belonging
In a place it has always belonged

The body it inhabits

The land where golden poppies bloom
Where ice becomes a fog too thick to pass
and people snow sled across white sands
They are all of the wind
...and more
And more...
It released itself from its twisted ropes
both unveiling and retching its existence

Gusting as a gale
passing before a stammered crowd
Only a few caught its gaze

The air escaped its vessel
Circulating out of its confined space

An aeolian process freeing the remnants

Waves of light and air escaped where a heart
once was housed

Perhaps it was the wind
Perhaps it was the waves
of blue that spilt over the cracks

of the soiled and stained earth

That bore witness to the suffering
That connected the wind to every
aspect to its new life

Perhaps the wind was always a tornado
Or perhaps the wind needed to meet
Itself outside of its dormant walls

to clear falsities in its path
To destroy ideals stored
in the tissue of its past

and wash over it with love
and washed over Me with love

Maybe she freed the wind
Or maybe the wind was silenced air

Waiting to escape so I could see
That I am a tornado, a hurricane, and a sandstorm

But I am also breath and radiating particles
A child born on the marina
held in the arms of a woman who suffered
abuse like mine

who named me after a ray of light

I am the infant laughing in the seafoam sky
as her father lifts her towards the clouds

I am the person that is both he and she
who loves a woman who both frees and shatters
my heart each time we kiss

I am the rainbow in reflection and refraction of myself
I am the red-earth of my ancestors
waiting to be shaped

I am the wind talker listening for
the winds harmony

As it smooths out anvils in the sky
pulling clouds closer to earth
reminding my toes they are touching tile

That she is lounging amongst the tiles
of my puzzled heart

Her golden hair cascading down
her blue jean jacket

I am here

I am here eating avocado toast
in the backyard patio
watching the chickens cluck and play

I am here

I am here to hold her
when she feels broken

I am here to kiss her eyelids
when the wind is spinning round

sending her somewhere deep

where she dissipates like condensation
of warm breath on a brisk winter's night

When she hides in the well of her memories
Where she huddles with the tears of her
little girl self

I am the person waiting to hold the
girl who is stuck at the bottom of the well
of her past

I am the one holding out my hand
waiting for her to grab on

I am waiting for her to see her power
I am waiting for her to see she is the wind
so that she will free herself
And I will climb down in the tenebrous well
to sit with her

Until she does

Bound to the Earth

Blood red Earth pressing into
The soles of my feet

Where is she? I wondered.

I had never been so bound
By my past as I was rooted
Under that evening's moon

My mouth redacted
My body covered in dry
Cracks of Mother's history

Some go to extremes to let go

She may never show, I concluded.
Then she walked into the room
Only this time she and everyone

Were looking
    At me

Lunchbox Message:

Small Spaces

I want to be in those seemingly
Meaningless small spaces
You know the ones

The ones between our grasping
Hands and between our palms
Where everything is soft and warm

The ones between our breasts
When our bodies move to the Earth's
Music in the pouring January rain

The ones between the moments
When romance beats the cold
Puddles on asphalt, splashing feet

You know the ones…
Between your lips
Captured in your gaze

Lunchbox Message:

We Live in a Poem

She is the vibrating air in my Anahata
Green as spring springing from her eyes
Restless wind—
She wakes me in my dreams

As we stare at the swirls of pinks purples and blues
Cascading in the sky like acrylic ink poured
Across a treated canvas

The wind rests upon my shoulder and brushes
Against my breast her breath rushes against my neck

As she encases me into the chasm
Of her body
She is both the wind and the earth
holding me tight
                    As if she wants me to stay forever
As if I belong

But I know that once the warmth of her lips
Touch mine she will flee
As quickly as air leaves my lungs

She will forever be the wind
Passing through my life
Bringing both warmth and chaos

I know that when she enters
We'll step into a vortex

Where the clouds gather and the sun
Gleams through like a spotlight

I will stand on the steps in awe of her
She will stand with her skirt flailing and spinning
About as the curls in her hair dance wildly

Her brilliant eyes speaking to my Anahata
I will know that I am home again

Only this time
I will release my storm
and dance with her
Perhaps we will kiss... but since we live in a poem
It will be more than
the flavor of our fervent words

The wind will sing and whistle
between the swaying sprigs of grass then
rustle in its alto tones amongst the clicks and
clacks of leaves
While the rain drops a beat
We don't need music
After all
Though her voice is melodic
and her hands flow with measure
We will dance to our own song—an aria
From the ripple of our wind language
While it isn't riddled with hums and quirks
of our twirling minds

And speaks from the hymns of our hearts'
Winds

I will know that she loves me because Mon Coeur

Will run her fingers over my cello strings
Where my air once strived
                                        and our souls will reverberate
                                                        Our poem

Moving Air

Cher Mon Coeur,

I am an air sign

born the year of the dragon
a fire dragon—to be exact—
and a Pitta in Ayurveda.

What does all this even mean? That I am a strong force of fire and air constantly moving—or I'll die? I don't know, I'm not even sure if I believe in any of this shit. I know that the heart chakra—the anahata—
is air and that when the wind begins whirling like the wings of a hummingbird you are always near. I know that as we dance on textured streams of the aurora borealis—under a clear violet sky invisible to our eyes—
that your skin is the scent of red-earth. As I pick at the ground digging up my clay to prepare my gift in solace to my hollowed svadhisthana—I feel like I am safe in your arms. But when I birthed my ghost the doctors held its diseased tissue in their hands—then announced its death—naming it endometriosis, and I was happy to never hold her in my arms.

Two years later a healer put me on her table under an orange sun. She told me that I never mourned the loss of my uterus. I felt that was ridiculous, but the silent air became a breeze and I saw white gold in my dreams as she placed her hands on my head—so I went home and wrote my uterus a letter. I received womb therapy several times—triggering the movement of memories streaming down my cheekbones, after the healer's hands dug deep into my sunken well. The healer pulled out my ghost's remains and forced me to see my pain, then had me write myself a love letter. Those written words move like the limbs of trees creaking and cracking in the wind.

My ghost left me with the remnants of her nightmares inhumed in the lining of my uterus. Though sometimes I wonder if all the pain I carry is even mine. Sometimes I wonder if the disease lives in my DNA. Maybe, my ghosts are my ancestors searching for peace in the clay of my vessel—molding me from the inside out. Maybe, I am coded like a monarch butterfly destined to follow the plan of her ancestors.

But I wouldn't even know what that means, because all I have are their stories traveling from my superior vena cava. I am a code etched in a mitochondria going towards my destiny. I am an Indigenous American without a community, separated from my cultures, unsure of where I belong. I don't know of my borderlands or speak the multiple languages of my people like the *new mestiza* Gloria Anzaldua traversed the empowerment of her indigeneity, the flex of her bilinguality, and beauty and strength of her *cunt*. That doesn't mean I'm not a *new mestiza*, it means my Indigenous Chicanx grandparents were beaten for speaking words of farmhands and chattel slaves and people that smelt of the red-earth hidden in the calluses of their hands and feet. It means I had a great grandmother who was enslaved and kept in a boxcar.

I'm curious of the stories of the people before them. The ones who shared the myths of the earth. Sometimes I feel the air moving across the hairs of my arm and I know the wind is whispering a truth. I don't know if my ancestors spoke to the wind. I don't know if they understood the language of a tree, taught to them by saltwater fish— like the Yaqui. I don't know if they had prophetic warnings of colonizers or art made with beads or seal skin. I don't know if they lived in ancient cities, tipis, or igloos...I know haplogroups C1b, Q-M3, and A2j1. Locations of origins, not culture or beliefs or tales of the winds speaking through the leaves.

So I'll climb in the tree and listen for your story. Or maybe the wind is coming from my anahata...waiting to speak to other hearts, rambling its unintelligible garble, searching for the ones who speak its language.

Maybe your anahata is the only one whose wind knows its song. I sometimes wonder if your heart aches when I question if anyone loves me. Perhaps there was never a question—only fear of not belonging on soil that has always been my home. Maybe I feel abandoned…or at least I did before I sat near the cornfields listening to cicada scream, while watching the flicker of glowing insects rising up from lush green grass. Maybe as I sat in solitude peeling the rind from my orange, watching the specks of juice sputter into the air, filling up the room with its aroma, and watching the juice drip from my knuckles onto the pressed wood of my dorm room desk I contemplated the suffering that created me. Maybe, I finally left my need to research their pain and the why of the how I ended up in the hospital bed.

I read the words of Maya Angelou and cried about belonging. I cried about the double rainbow I saw crossing through the red canyons of the Hopi people after I dropped off my daughter... somewhere deep in the woods across the country—far from all her people—but only four hours from my desk. I cried because the part of me that was connected to her is gone forever and she doesn't even know. I cried because part of me runs wildly trying to find herself, searching for healing and belonging just as I do. Part of me wants to heal, because she witnessed my suffering and can't look back—and I can't blame her.

Then there is the wind of me who pushes out the memories and tells me to keep moving forward—or I will die. I know now that as the wind I belong everywhere and nowhere—over all landscapes—beyond the leaves of the trees and the curls of your hair—I belong *every place—no place at all.* So I fell in love with this vessel and carved the words into my limb. When I look at my reflection I see the women who created me, women much stronger than I could ever be. I see women educated by the wind and by their abuelitas who taught them to knead masa and soak cornhusks like mine taught me. I see the curls of my black hair, curves of my almond eyes, and the dip at the end of my nose and I know that I am from more than California, Arizona, New Mexico, and Alaska.

I am from everywhere and nowhere. I am from wherever I want to be.

Chapter 2

The Great Granddaughter of the Dawn

Lunchbox Message:
A Passenger of the Rising Air

Mon Coeur,

If the heart chakra is air
and I am an Aquarius
does that make my heart's voice
a gale?

I have learned to love the wind
since every time you are near
I feel you in a breeze long before
I see you with my eyes

Sometimes your scent of
lavender and lemons
hitchhikes its way over
from the pressure of the heat

Of the sun on the Earth's
surface and there you are
a passenger of the rising air

Illuminating

Fireweeds in the Wind

Once the fire was over the grey soot cooled and the orange and red of the embers faded into the sky like the flicker of fireflies on an Illinois' evening in July. Images of corn stalks and monsoons float away—the way silk cracked from a dry corn husk does. But Alaska holds memories of my father's strong brow, in the overhanging cliffs. The sweat from his forehead streaming over his supraorbital ridge, with the melting glaciers over precarious rocks—threats of an avalanche to the golden pools surrounding the chambers of his eyes. His nose sloping down to his broad mustache covered lips. There is a dusty toy polar bear, stained yellow with age, peering up through my memories with its shiny coal shaped eyes stored in a Rubbermaid box. It is reminiscent of a time I don't know. A time that my mother flipped through pictures of my father in his olive colored military uniform scaling glaciers, and stories of my first ride home from the hospital. Stevie Wonder singing "Isn't She Lovely" over the truck radio as they drove beside the beach chilly February afternoon. Now cool air from the glaciers burst with misty tingles on my skin— dancing with a polar vortex through my unfettered hair. The long green stems and rosy pink petaled fireweeds sway as they grasp the crystal condensations absorbing the sun's streams—breaking through the billowing clouds.

While winter grasps August's sun filled nights and straggling Canadian Geese migrate—giant bees spin their wings around paling pink fireweeds—like storytellers in deep seeded time capsules awaiting the next purge. The season of summer is short but abundant with fishermen and fisherwomen in wading pants and long-sleeved shirts—catching sockeye and daylight.

In California, everyone is rushing on the 10...the 210...the 60, and intersections of time to make more time, but in Alaska they have all the extra time people in traffic jams search for. But here they close shops by 5 and their eyes shut while the sun is still up at 11 and a vortex of winter becomes polarized, icebergs become glacial silt and grey cracked mud releases permafrost, because of that thing Americans refuse to call global warming.

On the first night a calm breeze took to life as a passenger and chased the night in an old dented brown car—searching for the light from the sun's winds, but the clouds kept them hidden. The air became still, and the night became mood less—with the soft sounds of wind leaving the lungs of two strangers on intersecting paths—for a moment.

We are too far from the sun to hear its sizzles, crackles and pops, the way one might imagine Rice Krispies frying in a pan full of hot oil. Memories of ninth grade Outdoor Science Club experiments for NASA flash scenes of pouring rain in desert sands with warm taquitos fresh from the oiled skillet and into poncho hidden hands. It rained furiously and when the clouds passed the stars surrounded campers cradled by cliffs and cacti out in Joshua Tree. When the sun rose, we pulled out our equipment that we soldered chips and electric wires onto green boards. The cancelled space shuttle launch cultured disappointment but grew new discoveries in the recording of the rising sun, a lesson in rescue missions, and tracking trails.

Now here I am on an open highway chasing the Aurora Borealis, with melting snow streaming down mountain edges—like chasing the ends of rainbows with my mom in her car down suburban valley roads. I wondered if it was ever possible to see either. I wasn't disappointed by either adventure when I didn't get to find what I was looking for. Somethings were never meant to be. I knew that I would eventually see the Northern Lights, just like I once rode through the end or the beginning of a double rainbow. It was vibrant and clear through the dust of the red canyons where the Hopi people lived—even after letting go of my daughter—knowing she was planning on leaving me forever. I cried while the remaining particles of my heart both fell to my feet and lifted towards the sky.

I didn't know what was to become of me then, just as I don't know now that the fire is finally done burning.

I know that the fireweeds are blooming and that their leaves are turning soft pink. Soon they will whiten and dry up and the ground will be covered in snow—in Alaska. As for me... the flowers are vibrant in my memories, and I feel myself being pulled in many directions—but I hear the wind calling me towards the sun.

Desert Shark

In the desert I found a shark. Its cartilage was made of felt and peered at me through its mouth. It walked with legs and moved with the swirling cacti. Electrifying colors danced around on stage as the drum roll played, then a woman picked up her guitar and began to sing and the shark said it reminded her of her childhood.

The desert shark announced a trick that we would play. I would put on her head and find a stranger to dance with. I didn't know who was gay, so I asked a man instead. We twisted and twirled on concrete, just under a tree. Nothing magical. He wasn't the wind that wrapped around me and blew through me—like a ghost.

A camerawoman ran up...or was that a woman with a cell phone? Laughter ensued, as we ran to the bar. We crammed into a small room with more than 100 people—piled on the floor—while we sat at a long row of tables. Then the desert shark joined us as we listened to one of the most beautiful voices in a rickety wood paneled room—with a dirty faded and chipped green piano pressed up against the wall. The lights glowed on the singer's face and I began to sweat from the warmth of the crowd's breath, but my heart was relieved at least for a moment as the desert shark pulled out her phone and recorded the man performing. I took a deep breath and felt the wind enter my lungs, she sat on my heart again—Mon Coeur still had the pieces.

But when the desert shark was ready, she put on her driving hat and we popped in her car. That's when I mumbled and bumbled—with my eyes drooping shut—about how the wind was gone and I could no longer feel its cool kiss in the desert where harry legged tarantulas hatch and the dirt chips like paint on a faded green piano.

I imagined the crisp Alaskan sky and swirls of the sun's winds whispering to the magnetic field in the earth's atmosphere. I wanted to know what it said. Did the sun's plasma sizzle and pop as it funnels earth's particles—like it does in the morning as it gets out of bed and stretches its rays? Its pinks and greens swimming softly in a hum above the snowcapped mountains. I was cool but my words spilt out on the dash, and the desert shark said, "I'm sorry."

SOLAR FLARE BENEATH CARTILAGE

1…2…3…4…5…
plasma seeping from
my costal cartilages like
a slender thread of energy
whizzing through my thoracic
cage—flaring solar storms from
the sun's corona breaking out
from my seemingly stable shell
plunging me back to earth at a million
miles per hour

GINA DURAN. (HIDDEN DREAMS). CHARCOAL AND GOUACHE. 2021.

(Hidden Dreams)

Wild flowers pressed upon rusted memories
Of barred Dreams   relentlessly rising towards
Smoldering clouds as thick as smog and dusted crops
Across the Mexican border   past California
Clouds containing cash and egos not hopes for futures
                (Not chests of hope)
Hearts pounding with fluttering glee
Flee with pounding hearts towards fences
Burying Dreams in sand beneath the bordered weeds
Weeded (out) for their Dreams
Hidden deep   Left out to dry like the dying
Brittle dreams turning gold beneath the sun
Hidden deep (are their roots) from searching
Eyes as they Dream of the skies
Awaiting
The storm to pass   to enrich the soil
Escaping fears of being   Uprooted

And when it does   there will be growth
Lush with poppies   golden as the sun
Rich with Dreams that escaped the seasons

Golden State Roots

While affluent members of society
Wallow in worries of the uprising starving people
Who clean toilets and pick oranges

With their sun browned flesh
And native golden state roots
Spreading themselves and breaking

Rocky asphalt on every street corner
With the scent of toasted corn tortillas
and supple lengua mixed with cilantro

And cervezas   Ready to sit on dank
concrete floors and iron cages
I waft in memories of lavender fields
And lemon trees   as if Mon Coeur will set me free

Whispering Heat Waves

The sun has laid me to rest
under the crisp blue sky
Clouds floating by

Not a tornado in sight
I feel like I am cooking on a downdraft
under the ultraviolet rays near a plastic
swan floating by as I cool in the desert pool

The heat waves are all that speak to me
But this happens whenever
Something is wrong
only this time I have grown bored

So I swam in the pandemic
I dipped myself in chlorinated water
cleansing the silence of the space between

us

Now that the tornado is gone
I notice how much quieter it is
my hands are often in the earth

amongst worms and chocolate-
mint leaves lavender sage prickly
pear and summer squash plants

The world is on fire
It's not a hurricane or a tornado
But even the heat waves play its hymn

protesters are being teargassed and shot
with rubber bullets and more

Death

The seeds are being planted
I watered them before I left

The sun is speaking to us even now
that winter passed
Just wait and listen and maybe

You will see it is the sky pulling
itself apart from the seams and the light
will swiftly play across the arid landscape

Lunchbox Message:
Protecting the Stars from Light

You must be relieved to be released from
the heat of the sun

It's too hot for human life, so I don't know why
I put you there

I remember looking up at you from shavasana
with light

reflecting off your golden hair
undulating

like electrically charged particles meeting
Earth's atmosphere

Your soft skin bearing a smile
like an angel

but even the sun's winds float away from
the pressure

Maybe that's why you thought you needed
to protect me

Maybe that's why I thought I needed
to protect you

But if we protected the universe from the light
of stars

we would never see the energy of four
forms of hydrogen nuclei

compressed into helium rapidly slithering through
atoms of Earth's

unstable thermosphere like an illuminated
amoeba

pulled by magnetism like lovers dancing
in the sky

Hope in the Dark

Once the tornado passed, everything collapsed in on itself and the particles settled into darkness. The night sky seemed to have sat upon the ocean for at least thirty, maybe forty years. Where does time go anyway? This construct that tells us all when to rise, eat, shit, pray, and sleep. Why does the prayer time of monks—who have long died—dictate when and how I work, play, and love?

It is said that prayer is powerful.

Apparently so powerful it controls prana. So powerful that time is a cage compressing dreams between the folds of reality. Turning the complexity of past, present, and future into a seemingly linear stream flowing straight into death. But time is more than that. The present does not exist without the past or the future or even the light imbued by the stars in flux. Dust from chunks of fragmented stars impregnating the earth created our past as they folded in and birthed themselves, once again.

Now that everything is coming to an end, I feel the beginning. The past is meeting the future and I feel the wind, who has been speaking through the hurricanes and tornadoes, approaching. It is coming from my ancestors—they speak through the wind of the hummingbirds' wings. They come from the Sun.

The Compression of What Matters

/

The cafeteria was clamoring with a cacophony of clanking dishes and voices, so I studied in my room. Orange juice spattered as I dug my thumbs into the thick rind of my lunch. The sweet acidic scent fluttered up with a mist of despair. Little orange colored puddles formed on the oak patterned pressed wood of my desk. My books were on rape, sex trafficking, and children of color being sold into sex trafficking. The puddles of orange began to mix in with the puddles of my tears. I looked out over Urbana-Champaign from the top floor of my dorm and saw traffic that reminded me of a slow day in Fontana.

Another one of the many giant bucket dumping storms of the day was heading closer in a dark evening cloud—with a flash of purple and blue. I looked at my phone and saw breaking news about children locked in dog kennels, with shiny metal blankets, and cold concrete floors to sleep. This is what happens in America—home of the free, land of the brave. Is it brave to kidnap immigrant children escaping trauma and allowing them to be molested and herded into chain linked cages?

/

Not even the sun can contain its wind as it fuses hydrogen and helium. The compressed energy of our masses will release into the earth and everyone with a clear sky will see the light as the elements become one with our atmosphere.

Time dissolved until the words in books became so physical that their actions painted me into a latex cocoon. Its skin hugging my skin—naked in truth—until I pressed my thumbs into the layers of my peeling skin and pried myself from what was left of my memories. I left my shedding to fossilize on the reddened earth—stained with my blood and pubic hair—under the fabric spray painted swirls of the Aurora Borealis.

Transitions create hunger for love, friendship, food, and more change. Change that can only be found outside of the safety of your arms. The last time you held me we were standing in the streaming streetlights. If I had known that was the last time...
/
In Mexico, I trudged with friends [bound to reunite families] through something that looked like water but smelled like the sun boiling garbage clogging up a septic tank. I feel like god might stick its thumbs through the smog and tear a hole into the sky—but maybe it's time…

Rats and roaches scurried through a makeshift kitchen with boards around an outdoor sink. Crates with produce were piled precariously under the outdoor sink and stacked in a dank windowless room. Tents shoved in rooms that weren't meant to be rooms, roomed children separate from adults. A woman running the shelter said children are more susceptible to respiratory infections and spreading illnesses to adults. The smell of the water began to swim in the stench of pig shit and sweat, mixed with the malodor of racism and xenophobia dripping from the church walls wading in homelessness and death.

All I have to give is art.
/
Borders are black holes collapsing dreams—absorbing light from refugees—causing a calamity of collapsing stars. Soon they will merge nameless in the chaos, like the recent emergence of

two black holes—reverberating the universe—GW190521—because change is inevitable.

What happens when power compresses human lives, as if they don't matter? What happens when light is pulled into a confined space? If a corpse of a star can become more powerful than elements once illuminating light—now bending the fabric of space-time...

Hydrogen, helium, carbon, nitrogen, oxygen, neon, iron, silicon, magnesium, and sulfur.

Gravity in a black hole is the thumb of the universe, ripping space-time fabric apart. The black holes are without names, but their vibrations leave an echo—named GW190521.
/
Nameless: 76,020 unaccompanied refugee children crossed the border in 2019—52 percent higher than in 2018. 1,475 children went missing. 6 children have died—nameless. Their echo will be heard and named.
/

Why Toilet Paper?

Canada's snow chasm streets clung to my boots and told me to stay. I felt safe, for once. Yet, I knew no one, but the familiar kiss of the arctic wind on my California cheeks. My black hair shone under a fluffy cap made of snowflakes. I opened my mouth and stuck out my tongue to feel the ice flakes melt in my warm mouth. I suddenly had thick braided pigtails and Hulk pail in hand—I was 4 again. Then the flakes dissolved, my hair grew thin, and I had my leather backpack. Strangers greeted me and we chatted about where we were from. For once, I was a stranger in a foreign place, rather than being a foreigner on the soil where I was born and raised. Everyone could tell I was a Latina here too, but now it wasn't good or bad. I belonged in a place I never belonged. Strangers told me I should stay and that I was beautiful.

I stopped feeling beautiful—or really anything—the day my daughter sat at a large, pressed wood table in her counselor's office, with a grin. At least it looked like her. Suddenly the earth began to quake, and I was floating. Perhaps, the sun's gravity pulled all its gasses inward and our universe was about to collapse in on us. Maybe, the planets were about to spin out of order and fling into another galaxy. Now I would have to learn all new constellations and search for Polaris. My wife found a secret chart—several of them—in fact. Although, she would say it was me who left her.

Maybe she was right. Maybe someone else tried me on, like a coat. I don't really know, but a gale forced the doors to the room open—scattering our wreckage—and none of us returned home. My eyes were cracked like the windshield of a totaled car, while my daughter drifted deep into the woods. But many of her belongings sat in my garage—in boxes marked Mercedes' Shit.

And that's how I knew Mercedes wasn't coming back.

So, I gathered everything I could and cleaned up the mess. I practiced breathing until a tornado swooped me up from the mangled mess into her vortex and I became more. Until I finally found myself giggling and lying in the snow in la Gay Village, making snow angels on the ground of the street art exhibition, *Toiletpaper*.

Who knew that a month later I would spend weeks searching for toilet paper during a pandemic?

Her Fierce Warrior Heart

There was a red throated hummingbird lying limp on its side—in my path. The wind escaped me. I dropped to my knees staring at its shimmering Aurora Borealis in its feathers. Its beak pointed towards the road. Puddles formed in the corners of my almond eyes and all I could do was scoop it up with the leaves from my yard. Then I asked my son to help me give its death purpose—under the white jasmine stars and luscious green vines.

I thanked it for its beauty, love, laughter, and joy and hoped that its soul would rise towards the marmalade colored mass of hydrogen and helium in our caterpillar shaped solar system. I hoped that it transformed with the rest of us as time paused and wrapped back again. We would meet again soon, as we all are becoming something new. I knew the hummingbird would find the sun's wind swirling around the earth's sky and it would find its way home with its fierce warrior heart.

My son tells me that the Aztec sun god, Huitzilopochtli, is a hummingbird and that all his fallen warriors come back as hummingbirds. He has learned that we might be Aztec Nahua. I imagine this as I cover its shimmering wings with dark fertilized soil. I wonder whose spirit I lay in power. A breeze whispers a secret in my ear—my anahata rests in the cradle of my cracked ribs. The leaves in the trees began to dance as the sun held me in its rays. I could feel a zephyr of breath release in response. My heart was safe and soon I would stand outside the window of my grandmother's bedroom—with my n-99 mask—as my uncle and aunt held her. My uncle placed his hand on her forehead as he knelt to the ground in prayer. He prayed for her safe return home and gave thanks for her life. Normally, a priest would say her last rites—but those are times before COVID-19. I watched, then closed my eyes and meditated. I focused on my grandmother's light. I wanted her to know that I was also there for my mom and that she didn't have to fight to stay any longer. My mom knew my grandma loved her. My mom would always love her mom.

My eyes opened to see two of my grandma's children hold her while the wind from her body floated up towards home—like gravity fusing elements in a star. Every time I tell people she left this place I will say but not from COVID—not because they asked—but because I don't want to hear the question. I watched my grandma's mouth move with the air, as if to say I love you. It will never be the last.

Perhaps, her wind is part of the sun's—cascading into the earth's atmosphere in green, pink, and purple lights. Perhaps, she will live every time the Dodgers crack a baseball past the outfield and the stadium roars from cheers and jeers. Perhaps, she will live as we drink Pepsi and eat chicken enchiladas. Perhaps, she lives in her four children that she raised on her own—after my grandfather passed—or in the homes she bought by working two jobs. Perhaps, she is in the garden with her big floppy hat, pulling weeds. Perhaps, she is in our kitchens, teaching her grandchildren and great grandchildren how to make New Mexico chili while sniffling and sweating from the spices. Perhaps, she is taking care of our babies while we are away. Perhaps, she is listening and showing up when nobody else is around.

But I can tell you this, my Grandma Clara is a warrior. As I sit in my garden under a dark blue umbrella, a red throated hummingbird twirls its wings past my head. Then spins around to look at me. She rests her feet on my watermelon plant's stand and stares back at me. I say hello and smile, my heart pulling closer to my Vishuddha with excitement—fusing into a poem. I think now my grandma is home and now she gets to be in everything and in all of us. My grandmother wasn't Aztec, but perhaps today, she is staring back at me with her fierce warrior heart. Telling me she loves me. We will meet again soon, as we all are becoming something new.

Stolen Wind

The thick sepia stained air spilt onto the sun the color of burnt orange seeping through clouds of billowing smoke. I wandered out to raining ash and cooled ember puddles on my bare toes to attempt to play in my garden and talk to my plants. Normally, the lavender and sage swim in the scent of redwood chips, but today the stale sun ferments under the sapor of soot and seasons the soil with the flavors of Redlands, California. Not because the sun was so hot it rotted, withered, and singed the fruits of our labors, or even because some careless camper forgot that campfires are hazardous in the aired summer heat. No. A puff of blue shot out to reveal the news of some child's genitalia. A child who will forever remember that their families' repugnance destroyed 20,000 acres of wildlife. And they weren't the first.
Why?

Ignorance and hate are burning down the country with their constructs. Gender, sexuality, xenophobia, racism…

Breonna Taylor, was murdered in her sleep
and no one did a thing. Her wind was stolen.
The police officer was punished for shooting
a bullet through a wall. The wall received restitution.
It will rest in peace. It was probably white.

George Floyd's last words were *I can't breathe—*
while his wind was crushed by racist Blue Life.
I have yet to meet a Blue person, but I hear
their lives matter every time a Black person
is murdered by one.

White supremacists, militia, and anti-vaxxers
stood with shotguns in red, white and blue—
the country reopened.

Ahmaud Arber Was chased, beaten, and gunned down—
never to feel the breath of the sun again.
The raging fire scorched the earth because
Black football players can't kneel during the anthem.

The Navajo are suffocating from COVID-19.
Their lungs deprived of air for their ancestors
Who breathed as they walked before
the soil was colonized.

Brown and Black bodies are gathered in a pile, hung in trees, sex trafficked, stolen...

But soon no one will suffer in cages or lie on the street in their broken vessel of bones, the choice of life has been cut from the bodies of non-white women. Forced Sterilization. Eugenics. Genocide. Genocide is the fire ignited at the parties of racists. Dead people don't celebrate gender reveal parties. And Queer and Trans people celebrate coming out after they shed their forced gender roles.

When I see the slinky swirling movements of the Aurora Borealis dissolving and transforming like watercolor on a black canvas sky, I think how beautiful it must be to be without borders. How beautiful it must be to exist through an electromagnetic pull—becoming one with the universe and the earth—where all the colors exist in a symphony of light.

Lunchbox Message:
The Dawn of a Sangha

Sometimes, I want to lay in the wind to feel
its arms wrapped around me again

Because sometimes, I still smell the aroma
of you in the flowers and the trees.

Sometimes, I want to become the particles of the
solar wind and wrap my rays around Earth

Because sometimes, my poems are dreams
wrapped up in memories of you.

Sometimes, I want to be the flames of stars so
someone will see me. I had hoped it was you—

Because when I stood in the dark with my sister and son—
I wished your hand were holding mine.

Sometimes, I want to whisper all my secrets to
you—then I remember that you are the wind

Because you are always moving, and I am
the great granddaughter of the dawn.

I am of the sun and I am the electrically charged
particles of my dreams and you…

You are more than the wind or the earth, you are
my friend who held me until my words became

Poems and letters became love messages on
walls and paintings became nightscape dance

floors within the aurora and you became more
than a love story in a book of my dreams.

You became sangha, and that is how this poem
begins...

NOTES

The biggest contribution to my research on wind and tornadoes was from *Tornado Alley*, by Howard B. Bluestein, who went gave in depth descriptions of wind and cloud formations. I also found a great deal of inspiration from The Fusion Quest, on fusion process of the sun, and to help with my understanding of the aurora borealis for the second half of the book. To extend my lessons on the aurora borealis I read Northern Lights: The Science. Myth, and Wonder of Aurora Borealis, as well as traveled to Alaska in the summer and winter to try and observe the lights. I was able to see faint lights in February but missed the big spectacle due to the pandemic.

My greatest inspiration of love poetry and discovery of self was Adrienne Rich's *Twenty-One Love Poems* and *Diving into the Wreck. Twenty-One Love Poems*, particularly XIII, was the first love poem ever given to me and I started writing *Lunchbox Messages* to Mon Coeur a few months later. (Not all of those poems made the last cut.) *Diving into the Wreck* taught me a lot about telling a story and creating a moment through metaphor. It also helped me learn how to combine many separate moments into one story.

Finally, *Legal Codes and Talking Trees*, by Katrina Jagodinsky helped me find poetry, mythologies, and prophies from Native American culture that helped me express the questioning of my ancestor's culture. It is not my culture, but I respect the Indigenous people living and surviving in America where I understand what it is like to have my culture stripped away even though I am incapable of knowing mine.

REFLECTIONS AND REFRACTIONS OF MYSELF

I began writing this book as a series of love poems that I intended on calling Lunchbox Messages for the one I call Mon Coeur—which began during a time of sadness—which had so many more beginnings and endings before that. I wanted to be able to discuss those beginnings and ending, which was often wrapped up in trauma, without being as overt and literal as I was accustomed to writing. My art was literal, my poetry was literal, and my words were literal. This was the beginning of a new artistic freedom for me. Although, I prefer to be a truth teller, I felt like I wanted to speak in metaphor like one of my favorite poets, Adrienne Rich. I think that I could easily say that most of my poetry was inspired by Rich's "Twenty-One Love Poems" and "Diving into the Wreck"—which I'll get into in a bit. After I graduated from Chaffey College, I took a few English Literature courses at Mount San Antonio College, where Mon Coeur convinced me to keep Mexican American Literature. (I didn't think I was going to get anything out of it, because I felt so acculturated that I had developed almost a resentment to it—even though I wanted desperately to reconnect. This is where I discovered the enchanting style of magical realism. It was in Contemporary Mexican American Literature that I saw that I still had many things in common even though I didn't come from Mexico or speak Spanish. But maybe, finding one's self when there is generational trauma and assimilation is about reconnecting with cultures that we never really had the pleasure of knowing. Maybe, this is all a symptom of colonization.

My goals for this collection were to learn how to express more works where I become a character other than myself (the wind), as well as explore things through dream states and metaphorical language. I wanted to be able to use the techniques in magical realism—which are more often found in contemporary Mexican American literature—in order to keep some of my personal life more private. Although this really posed as a challenge for me since I am used to writing creative non-fiction and poetry from more literal perspectives. I often had to remind myself that it was okay for me to exaggerate and essentially create a new world where my truth was hidden in metaphorical meaning. I get stuck when I feel as though not being literal is not being honest. In reality, I am speaking the truth but describing feelings and moments for those outside of my head to possess a deeper understanding of something they may not have ever experienced. I realized how much research must go into fiction writing in order to create well-developed and multifaceted characters. Even though my poetry is not based on fiction, it was still necessary for me to learn a great deal about different types of wind and how the environment is altered by it.

Tornado Alley, by Howard B. Bluestein helped me see the poetry in anemology and meteorology. When describing different cloud formations Bluestein states, "The cumulonimbus, also known as a cb, needn't produce thunder and lightning, although sometimes it does. With its nearly vertical sides and smooth anvil tops, cumulonimbus clouds often resemble magnificent works of art sculpted by the wind" (Bluestein 23). I truly loved the description of smooth anvil tops and used the phrase in my poetry. Other terms that helped me describe emotional conflict and barriers of growth were words like tropopause, Bluestein explains "The tropopause acts like a ceiling to growing clouds. If there is no vertical wind shear, the top of the cloud, which is composed mainly of ice crystals, spreads out like a pancake to form what is called an anvil" (Bluestein 17). To help further explain the formation and spreading of the anvil shaped tropopause Bluestein describes updrafts, which he says are "so strong that they have enough kinetic energy to punch through the tropopause before they collapse" (Bluestein 20). I found this strength and kinetic energy to be a positive and powerful force capable of bursting through the negative downdraft of my character's childhood and adult trauma—which I felt best to describe as a tropopause.

Some of my research went outside of the library such as sitting in the wind while surrounded by the rustling trees, to record them on windy days. Then other days I spent researching hurricanes online through sciencing.com, where I learned about the Coriolis effect, "a phenomena where the rotation of a free-moving object such as wind is influenced by the spinning Earth. Wind in the Southern Hemisphere moves to the left. This is why the circulation of cyclones forms opposite rotations in the right and left hemispheres" (Sciencing). This not only spoke to my love of my ninth-grade advanced science where I was first introduced to physics, but an acknowledgement to my Fluidity and Art Intersection course, at Harvey Mudd. I wanted to recognize my time learning with Prof. Levy, because she taught me more about math than any educator (or my parents) before her—through art. Plus, it helped to explain the separating of the self when an opposing force came into conflict (which also happened to be myself)—or in other words: when I struggled with my past and desire to live.

Another challenge that I came across was explaining my cultural conflicts. In my Power for Social Change class I learned that within the definition of culture that Americans do not actually have a culture. This was disheartening, because my culture was not really shared with me due to the Mexican and American "conflict". Many of the members of my family were punished for speaking Spanish and had already lost their culture from the genocide of Native Americans. Since my ancestors are from three different Native American nations, I do not have a culture—I have Catholicism—a tradition I left. I have been curious as to why some family members continue to follow their Catholic beliefs—considering lifestyle and low church attendance. My issues with this are apparent when I introduce my character The Apple Temptress, who struggled with her desire to believe in God while snorting crystal meth, which was first introduced to her by her uncle. I found this to be an interesting connection in my poetry, because I experienced abuse as a direct result of my uncles who used crystal meth and steroids. I watched childhood friends drop out of school—who later told me it was because of drugs that they bought from my uncles. I grew up seeing alcoholism/abuse of alcohol and violence within my family structure. I wondered often if dysfunction was my culture. Dysfunction that was more than likely from generational trauma.

Native Americans have an epidemic of drug and alcohol use within their nation states, but I find it interesting that my families have similar backgrounds. Even though one side grew to believe that they were Mexican Americans and the other Hispanic, they assimilated to American culture—when both have Native American ancestry and show symptoms of what I describe "as an extreme assimilation responses," in my research Sexual Violence and the Assimilation Response of LGBTQ2 Female Identified Latina and Indigenous Americans for the University of Illinois Urbana-Champaign—including suicides and attempted suicides. Although I am no longer ashamed of my attempt and I have discussed my cousin Rachel's suicide at length for art and research, I feel it is better to describe these moments and feelings through techniques like surrealism and magical realism—to help blur the lines of truth, imagination, and emotions. The fact is that when many people are suicidal those lines are blurred and things can feel unreal and disjointed. I did not have a concrete way of describing my emptiness and inability to belong from my lack of culture, so I looked for research on Native Americans and the sounds of the wind, because it fit my criteria and my curiosity about a belief that there are people who can talk to the wind—much like some healers or medicine (wo)men are often able to speak to spirits or relate prophetic dreams. I was not able to find anything on wind talkers or speaking to the wind. All I have are Native American proverbs like, "Listen to the wind, it talks. Listen to the silence, it speaks. Listen to your heart, it knows." Yet, I do not even know if it actually is a Native American proverb because it circulates on the internet, so I found another point of interest: trees.

Legal Codes and Talking Trees, by Katrina Jagodinsky gave me poetry from other Native American women who were also trying to maintain their culture and not assimilate. I found this to be very inspiring but was more interested in their prophecy about the talking tree. Jagodinsky explains a myth of a talking palo verde tree that spoke to the Surem (Yaqui or Hiyaqui Yoeme) people before the time the borderlands were formed due to the Spanish conquest. After what seems to have been many attempts by the Hiyaqui Yoeme wise-men—the Hiyaqui Yoeme people appear to have agreed that nobody could make sense of "the buzzing words repeated in the branches" (Jagodinsky 1). This led the wisemen to seek the knowledge of twin girls who lived "on Grandmother's Mountain", who would set out on a journey to learn a new language spoken by the saltwater fish. Once the girls learned how to speak the new language, the saltwater fish were able to teach them how to interpret 'the strange messages' coming from the tree (Jagodinsky 1). These sounds were prophetic messages for the Hiyaqui Yoeme people, telling them of "the coming tide of conquest, colonization, and Christianity" of their people (1). I decided to make a reference to this portion of the book, because many of these people lost their culture through assimilation and religion—many probably became Catholic since the missions were constructed and ran by the Spanish who forced Indigenous Americans into Christianity and taught them Spanish as well as giving them Spanish names. For example, the Hiyaqui Yoeme became the Yaqui and then later Surem. Perhaps it was from difficulties with pronunciation, but I would like to do my best to respect the people who are connected to their stories and their culture.

I felt that even though I am probably not Hiyaqui Yoeme (on either side of my family)—even though my mother's side is from New Mexico and my father's side is from Arizona—as a person who photographs trees and listens to the wind move through the leaves that this prophecy would best help describe my disconnection from my ancestors.

Finally, Adrienne Rich stuck in my mind throughout the entire process because Diving into the Wreck describes her coming out process in completely metaphorical language. I aspire to write something as beautiful as she does and hope that people will analyze my story as much as I have hers—whether it is wrong or right. Adrienne Rich, transforms herself through metaphor by switching from a diver to taking the shape of the mythological mermaid—while also playing with gender norms as she becomes he: "And I am here, the mermaid whose dark hair/ streams black, the merman in his armored body" (Rich, 164). Her metamorphosis from human to mythical creature, exhibits her strength: while becoming both male and female—exemplifying her love for women, while acknowledging both genders within herself. Rich empowers herself by showing that she does not have to follow gender or societal norms, by diving deeper: "We circle silently/ about the wreck/ we dive into the hold./ I am she: I am he" (Rich, 164). I hoped to show this throughout my process as I expressed my female and masculine characteristics as the wind. Even at some points I was both an updraft and a downdraft, as well as hurricane and a sandstorm. I free myself from my binds during my inner and exterior struggle—where I finally find love. Since I often struggle with being more open with my gender fluidity, I wanted to write something that spoke to similar things as Rich did. Although my struggle was explicit, it is also about healing from sexual trauma I do not know if I could say Rich did not struggle from sexual trauma or even if forcing oneself to live as a straight person is not sexually traumatizing. It is described as 'coming out of the closet' and the only other thing described as being in the closet are our 'skeletons'—usually associated with trauma.

The second section of the book was originally meant to explore who I had become after these many tests of courage that I set for myself in the healing process, but nothing goes as we plan and I'm not sure if anyone would have planned for the coronavirus. Now I wonder what dreams really look like during the pandemic. The second chapter begins with poems about the evolution of my friendship with Mon Coeur and my first journey to Alaska. I think that as my healing and life evolve the relationship evolves with it. Yes, there were arguments, misunderstandings, and times to listen and learn like any other relationship, but I felt that in order to properly portray love we need to see that compromises and discussions were made and had. Without divulging too much of my personal life--particularly not discussing Mon Coeur's—I wanted to share how a loving relationship evolves as the people in it evolve.

As for the rest, I wanted to discuss how love and healing of the self is not just focused on the individual, but about the world and the other people around us. Self-love is spending time with loved ones and community (not just the taking care of ourselves as individuals); it is helping the homeless man eat and bringing art clothing to refugees. It is about loving everyone. Mon Coeur taught me how to love my enemy, but years of therapy taught me how to set boundaries. I teach empathy, introspection, and community building to homeless, LGBTQIA+, foster, and refugee youth. I teach these skills so that youth learn how to share their love and find and give community support, as well as to help themselves and others speak their truths. Homeless LGBTQIA+ have the second highest suicide rate in the United States, they also happen to have the second highest rate in experiencing sexual violence. Native Americans have the highest suicide rate in the United States and the highest to experience sexual violence. (This is not a coincidence.) Therefore, I make art, write, and do research on trauma and healing. It is imperative that this country makes changes, and many of the ways we can prevent suicide and sexual violence is through acceptance and support of those who are marginalized and oppressed. It is imperative that we create and develop community, empathy, and introspective transformation. Although, there is a huge misconception that empathy is about codependency and that introspection is about negative self-talk. I believe that with unlearning colonial ideals and furtherly developing new pedagogies, we can overcome these obstacles together. But first human constructs designed to oppress need to be dismantled, so I discuss much of what is happening in society today—especially during this pandemic. Writers like; Gloria Anzaldúa, Audre Lorde, and Maya Angelou helped me understand the concept of decolonization and the need to create new tools to reconstruct our society to reconnect with community and find sense of belonging. But first and most importantly, we all need to come together as One.

ONE[2]

I am One angry woman
Comprised from sexual violence
Compiled Contrived Compromised
By Construct
                    A Construct of human
                                    Ideals
Not reality
               Not Truth
But the need of Compartmentalization
          To obtain Power
Not for understanding

Queer Straight Brown Black White
               Male Female
                    Trans
Two-Spirit or One
          Human

I am One angry human
          Seeking healing
I am healing
          Seeking to heal
Prepared to heal
                    through empowerment

               As One

2 Duran, Gina. "One." Sexual Violence and the Assimilation Response of LGBTQ2 Female Identified Latina and Indigenous Americans. University of Illinois Urbana-Champaign. 2018. (pp 29). 2018.

WORKS CITED

Anzaldúa, Gloria. Borderlands/La Frontera: The New Mestiza. Aunt Lute Books. 1987.
Bryson, George. Northern Lights. Hall, Calvin. Pederson, Daryl. Sasquatch Books.
Seattle. 2001.

Duran, Gina. "(Hidden Dreams)". The Otherside Mag: The Revival Edition. (pp 41). 2018.

Duran, Gina. "One." Sexual Violence and the Assimilation Response of LGBTQ2 Female Identified Latina and Indigenous Americans. University of Illinois Urbana-Champaign. 2018. (pp 29). 2018.

… "Un-know." Sexual Violence and the Assimilation Response of LGBTQ2 Female Identified Latina and Indigenous Americans. University of Illinois Urbana-Champaign. 2018. (pp 13). 2018.

Fowler, T. Kenneth. The Fusion Quest. The John Hopkins University Press. 1997.

Rich, Adrienne. "Diving into the Wreck." The Fact of a Doorframe: Poems Selected and New 1950-1984. W.W. Norton. New York, NY. (pp 162-164). 1984.

... "Twenty-One Love Poems." The Fact of a Doorframe: Poems Selected and New 1950-1984. W.W. Norton. New York, NY. (pp 236-246). 1984
Smith, Andrea. Conquest: Sexual Violence and American Indian Genocide. South End Press. 2005.

Cover Art. Cover Photographer. Cover Photo Editor.
Gina Duran. *Dancing into Space-Time.* Collage Pop-Up. 2020.

I wanted to represent several aspects of my poetry in this piece; the aurora borealis (or solar winds), the vortex of wind that is an escape from our world, space-time, and the moment we danced on my 10'x12' painting of the aurora borealis. In my poem "Hope in the Dark", I talk about space-time and how, "The present does not exist without the past or the future or even the light imbued by the stars in flux." Since I perceive time as curved (and more cyclical than linear) I wanted to show the curves in space-time in the shape of the light of the solar winds swirling in an Alaskan night sky. When my character and Mon Coeur dance on the swirling paint in the poems I envisioned them entering a vortex where time does not exist, which I imagine as a tear in time, and as a place where anamnesis and precognitive dreams do not matter. The present moment is all that truly exists. The rest are memories that our brains perceive to be real. Then I asked myself: what is real if all perspectives differ? I felt like 2020 was the ultimate example of how people's realities of a country like America can be both "great" and terrifying. 2020 showed us how time varies depending on circumstances and how love and community can take new forms during times of uncertainty. It made me wonder what a tear in space-time might look like. Maybe a tear in space-time is the chaos of a pandemic and the distortion and understanding of time constructs create cultural shift. In other words, the world needs something massive like a pandemic to shift perspectives and to create change in society. Regardless, it is our choice as a society or collective whole to move towards new perspectives. By the time I finished the first chapter I chose to see my time here as a chance to heal and love¬—rather than exist in my anamnesis or destruction of my connection to the world. The character Mon Coeur is not only a representation of my love interest, but of love in general. Mon Coeur is when friendship, family, partnership, sangha (spiritual family), and community come together to heal and create a more viable present and future.

Gina Duran. *Collage of (Hidden Dreams*). Collage. 2021.

Collage of (Hidden Dreams) was made to accompany the poem "*(Hidden Dreams)*." Both the collage and the poem were inspired by Paul Buck's European Pressphoto of the border wall between Tecate, Mexico, and Tecate, California. When I wrote the poem *(Hidden Dreams)*, in 2017, I was beginning my research on detention centers and I wanted to describe my emotions about our future and the human suffering created by attempts to cross the border and escape the injustices largely caused by inequality and economic disparity. When I began my studies at Pitzer College I learned about the issues surrounding global food trade specifically those involving "Banana Republic", which was a term originally coined for Latin American countries whose economies were dependent upon the trade of bananas, such as; Honduras, Guatemala, Ecuador, Columbia, and Costa Rica. Now the term includes what is countries like Botswana and Bangladesh. Unfortunately, this economic model has caused so much disparity within these countries that it has resulted in food insecurities and a demand for child labor. This is one of the significant reasons why people from Latin American countries flee from their homes and become refugees - to find safety and food for their children. Meanwhile, we build shotty fences and call them walls to keep refugees and their children out. This fence does not do anything, it is a waste of taxpayers' dollars since most labor that American's refuse to do is often done by immigrants from the countries listed above. However, in 20011 the DREAM ACT (The Development, Relief, and Education for Immigrant Minors Act) granted temporary residency to these immigrants and would eventually grant permanent residency, under the condition that the minors of the "undocumented immigrants" attend college or serve the United States military. It is because of this acronym and economic and food deserts that I make so many references to dreams and being uprooted in my poem. This art and poem are my advocation towards the right to work and eat without discrimination in a country that has contributed to food deserts and economic upheaval. Where are people who have lost everything supposed to go when we are one of the largest contributing factors to their loss of income and resources? I dream of a safer future for immigrants.

www.ingramcontent.com/pod-product-compliance
Lightning Source LLC
Chambersburg PA
CBHW021741190726
48288CB00009B/3127
* 9 7 8 1 9 5 3 4 4 7 7 3 9 *